THE OXFORD PIANO METHOD

P·I·A·N·O T·I·M·E
S·I·G·H·T-R·E·A·D·I·N·G

B·O·O·K

3

Pauline Hall and Fiona Macardle

Music Department
OXFORD UNIVERSITY PRESS
Great Clarendon Street, Oxford OX2 6DP

Oxford University Press, Great Clarendon Street, Oxford OX2 6DP, England
Oxford University Press Inc., 198 Madison Avenue, New York, NY 10016, USA

ISBN 978-0-19-372770-0

24

Music originated by Seton Music Graphics Ltd., Ireland

Book design by Barbara Prentiss

Printed in Great Britain on acid-free paper by
Halstan & Co. Ltd., Amersham, Bucks

INTRODUCTION

Congratulations! You have safely pioneered your way through the hazards of Books 1 and 2, and now Book 3 lies ahead!

Your challenge in this book is to be able to do without the printed code-signs used in Books 1 and 2, but to do all your checking as if they were still there to remind you.

Here is a map with a message. Say it regularly to yourself and it will guide you through any panic stages.

And your
TWO GOLDEN RULES:

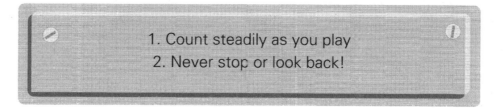

1. Count steadily as you play
2. Never stop or look back!

Remember the secret code-signs we used in Books 1 and 2? Here is a list of them to remind you. Get used to checking **everything** before you set off on each piece.

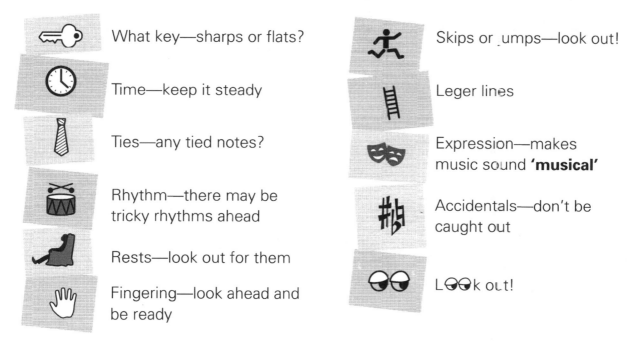

What key—sharps or flats?

Time—keep it steady

Ties—any tied notes?

Rhythm—there may be tricky rhythms ahead

Rests—look out for them

Fingering—look ahead and be ready

Skips or jumps—look out!

Leger lines

Expression—makes music sound **'musical'**

Accidentals—don't be caught out

L👀k out!

These code-signs will be at the beginning of each stage, so you may sometimes have to look back to remind yourself. Some of the pieces will have their own code-sign beside them as an extra reminder.

Measuring up

Have you ever looked at different maps and noticed that although the maps may be of the same area, the scale may be different? One may be large covering a whole page, whilst another may be small enough to fit into your pocket. Music can be a bit like this.

We're going to have a go at sight-reading in $\frac{3}{8}$ time. It's the same as $\frac{3}{4}$ except that instead of counting in crotchets, we count in **quavers**.

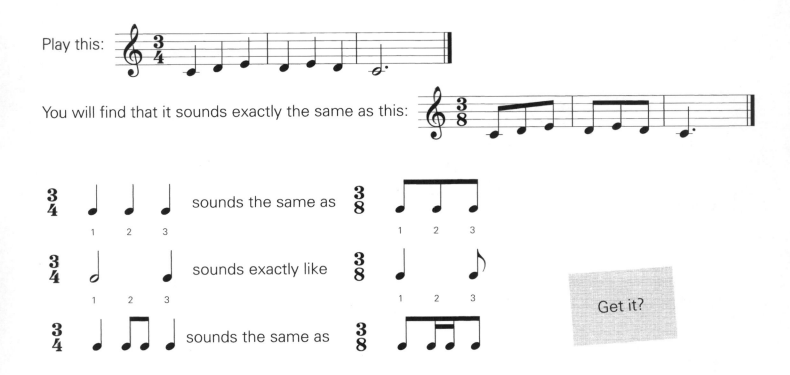

Play this:

You will find that it sounds exactly the same as this:

Get it?

Which of these pairs of tunes sound exactly the same? L👀K OUT!—there might be a catch!

3 🔑 L👓👓K OUT! This is a new key—D—with two sharps.

Remember that in $\frac{3}{8}$, ⅞ is **1 count.**

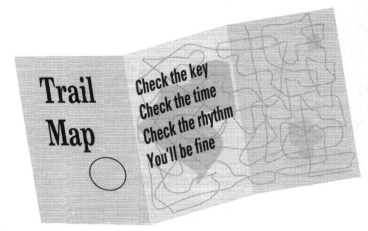

6   Count out two bars before you start to play.

7

8   Rests.

9

You should now be very familiar with this rhythm: $\frac{3}{4}$ 𝅗𝅥. ♪ 𝅘𝅥

Here's the same rhythm in $\frac{3}{8}$

Sometimes you'll find this rhythm: Can you work it out?

(It's very easy to get and muddled up. Always look out for the dotted note which will be the longest one.)

Here are two sound-alikes:

Now it's left hand's chance to venture out alone!

G·U·E·S·S AND P·L·A·Y

☞ *for two players* ☜

Scattered round the page are lots of short bits of music. They're all different. The aim of the game is to see if you can listen first and then spot the one that's just been played.

You need two players:

Player A — Shut your eyes and **listen hard**!

Player B — Play one of the tunes (twice).

Player A — Open your eyes and look carefully. Which one was played? Guess! Were you right? If so, well done!

Now change places.

Questions and answers

In this stage both hands have quite a lot to do, so plenty of careful looking and checking BEFORE you place your hands.

Some of these pieces are in 'question–and–answer' form, whilst some are 'chasers'. Look carefully. Try to bring out the tune even if it is in the left hand. Pretend you are playing these for an exam. An examiner might have heard these pieces played very badly at least twenty times already today. Give them a treat—make these pieces a pleasure to listen to!

1

Allegretto

2 ♭s in both hands.

3

Because you've collected so many code-signs, we're dropping three of them  but keep checking before you play, as if they were still there.

7 The last note in a piece very often gets cut short! Make sure you hold it on for its full value.

8

9 Check how many counts the rests are worth before you begin!  Which hand plays a black note?

10

11

A M·U·S·I·C·A·L W·O·R·D P·U·Z·Z·L·E

Have a little break and try out your word skills. There is a clue for each word which goes across. When you have completed these words you will find the name of something you know well, written in the middle column.

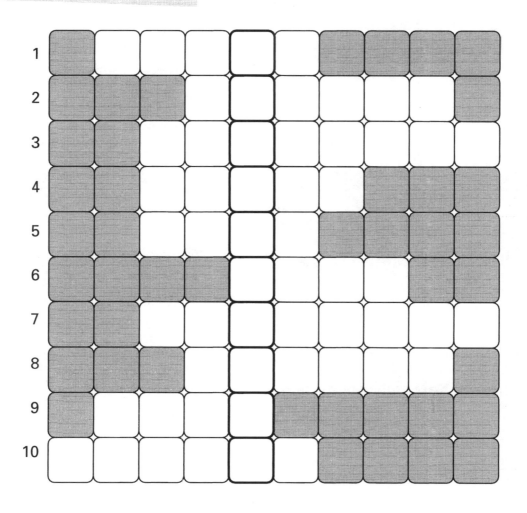

Clues

1   The Italian word for 'time'.

2   A stringed instrument.

3   How would you play this note? ♪

4   Slow.

5   A wind instrument.

6   ♭

7   ♩

8   𝄞 This is a _____ clef.

9   𝄽

10 ♪

Show time

By now you are more used to rests. This stage has six very short but pleasant pieces which you might like to play to someone else.

Get used to someone else listening to your playing—it can be quite nerve-racking, so plan each piece carefully and check everything in advance. Better still, also try to hear the piece in your head before playing it to your audience.

1

2 Don't confuse a **phrase-mark** with a tie. They look very similar, but a phrase-mark is over a group of **different notes,** and a tie is between **the same notes**—holding them on.

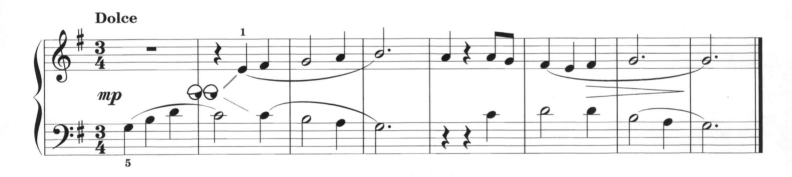

3

No more 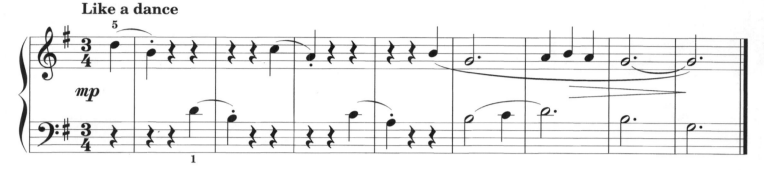 code-signs from now on but don't stop looking out for expression marks.
After all does mean something, and there is a great difference between *p* and *f*!

4 In a piece where there are lots of rests you must count out loud (even if it's only a whisper).

Like a dance

5 Double-check that you can do the right-hand rhythm in the second-to-last bar.

Andante

6 Any black keys? Which hand? Count out bar 4 carefully before you start.

Beware! Both hands off!

7 Imagine you're a teacher! Your pupil needs lots of help with sight-reading but the code-signs have somehow got left out in the next piece!

Draw the four signs that you think would be the most helpful:

Striding out

To some people, intervals bigger than a second can look the same. Look carefully at the examples below and compare them.

seconds

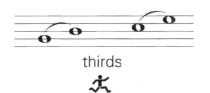

thirds

fourths

Test your observation

Go through the bars below and say, as quickly as you can, whether you think they are seconds, thirds, or fourths. Then go back and write the intervals below, checking as you go. Last of all, play them.

Check where the fourths are in the next piece before you begin.

1 👓👓 Any black keys?

2

Allegretto

Both hands off

14

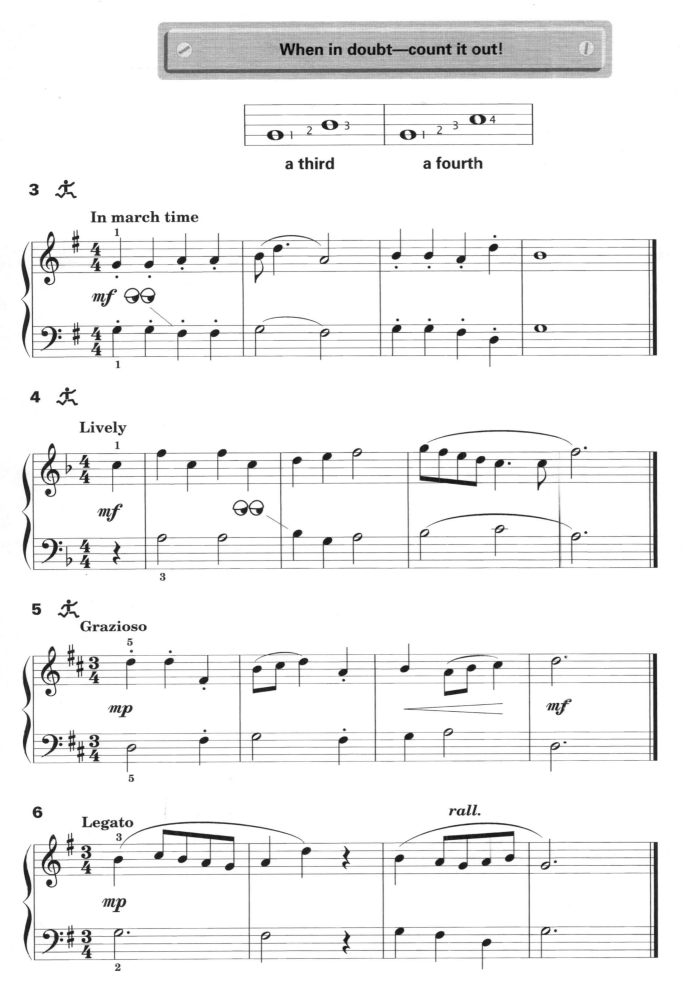

a third   a fourth

3

In march time

4

Lively

5

Grazioso

6

Legato   *rall.*

Are you remembering to check the key and time signatures
of **every** piece before you do anything else?

STAGE 5

Easy does it

Some of these are just a little more difficult.
Don't panic—prepare well!
Make sure you don't advance too fast into unknown territory!

1 👓 Lots of B♭s.

The next pieces are all in $\frac{6}{8}$ time—the first time you have come across this time signature.

It isn't difficult if you remember a few things:

- Each bar $\frac{6}{8}$ is only the same as two $\frac{3}{8}$ bars stuck together.

- Until you are happy with $\frac{6}{8}$ time count six quavers in a bar.

- Remember

- Be careful—a crotchet ♩ is worth  so you should look out for

2 👓

3 👓 F♯s.

Perhaps you know the next tune. L👀k out for the accidental in the last bar.

Can you convert the next 6/8 tune into 3/8 by adding some new barlines and changing the time signature? Play it first.

Play it again after it becomes 3/8 . Does it sound any different?

7 Don't forget a **quaver** rest ⅞ (it looks a bit like a funny figure 7).

Jumping for joy!

Once you can manage a FIFTH, other intervals seem easy!

You have already been using fifths in the bass—but from now on we use them and larger intervals for both hands. A fifth is just two thirds stuck together!

When in doubt—count it out!

a 'line' fifth   a 'space' fifth

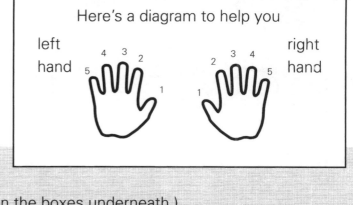

Here's a diagram to help you

left hand   right hand

Quick as you can—what are these intervals?
(Name them first, and then write the answers in the boxes underneath.)

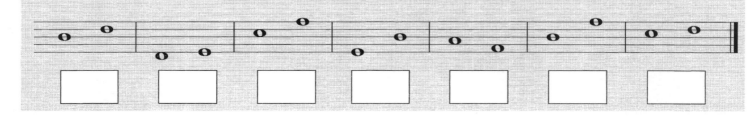

From now on we're leaving out the rest sign 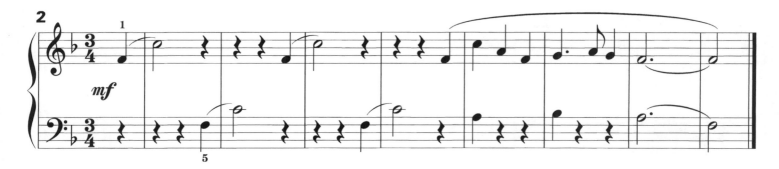 but this doesn't mean there are no more rests!

1 👓 Don't let left hand get caught out.

Marcato

f

2

mf

3

Andante

4 How many times does the left hand play F#?

Piacevole

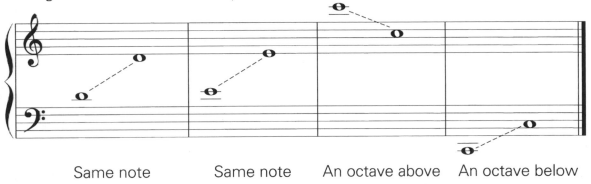

A quick look at LEGER LINES

These scare some people—but there's no need to be nervous of them.
Just get used to one or two important ones:

Same note   Same note   An octave above   An octave below

Quick as you can! Find and play these:

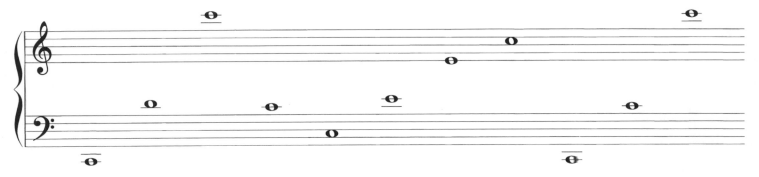

In the boxes below are some short music patterns. The game is to look at one for two seconds. Shut your eyes. Play it! Get your hand ready before you begin. Ready?

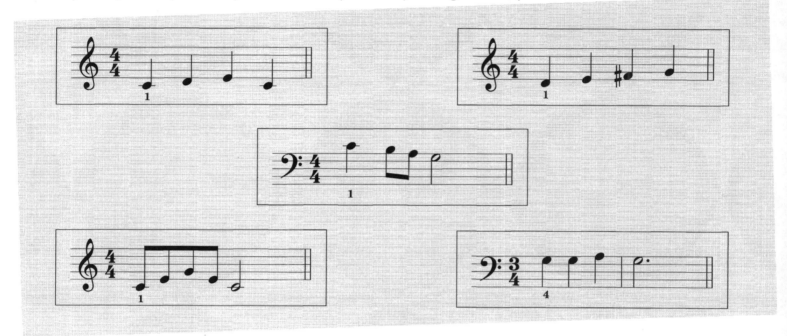

Now they're getting a bit harder!

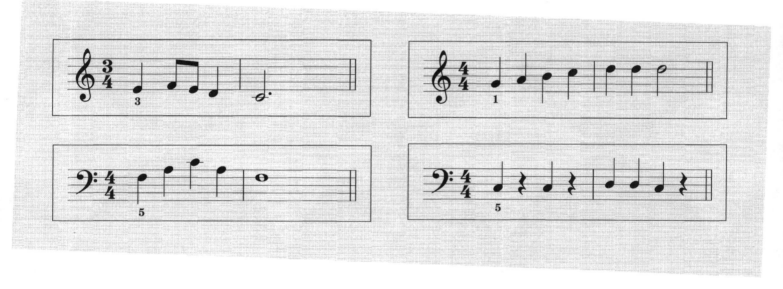

And a really difficult one! Give yourself five seconds to look (spot the way the notes are in a pattern):

You can try this memory game with any music.

Reaching out

At this stage, changing the position of your hands is probably the most frightening thing! Having been used to being in one place for the whole piece, your hand must move—sometimes once, sometimes more often. These moves are usually marked with fresh fingering. NOTE THEM WELL. Move your hand silently from one place to the other, once you have decided which hand is moving where!

Remember this code-sign?

Remember! If you find any of these pieces just too difficult, pencil in a reminder in the margin and ask your teacher to help you.

1

New hand position. Left hand moves down one note then stays.

2

3

One of the sneakiest ways to move the position of your hand is by the interval of a **sixth**. Your whole hand moves up one note which can be very off-putting if you forget that you've got yourself one step further up the keyboard!

A sixth looks like this:

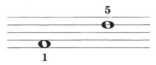

and there are four notes between your thumb and fifth finger.

Can you spot the sixths amongst this lot?

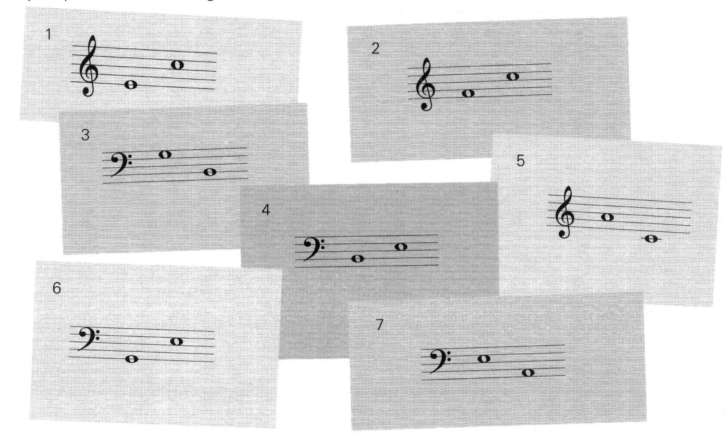

Do you recognize this tune?

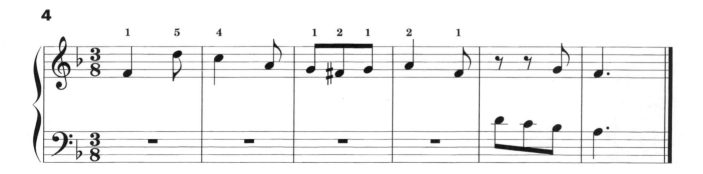

5 👓👓 In the last two bars the left hand has some big stretches.

6

7

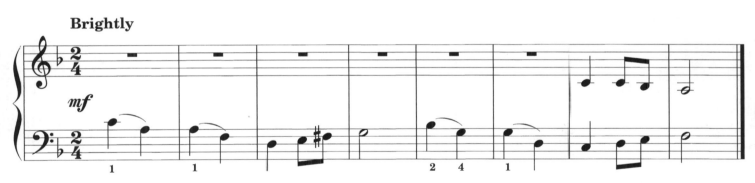

WELL DONE! That stage wasn't easy, but the trick is now to
go back and try to sight-read the pieces in the early books that
you didn't learn, and any other easy-ish music you can lay your
hands on.

There are so many pieces in this book you could even go back
and play them again. Then you will see just how far you have
come to reach this stage! NOW PLOUGH ON!!

STAGE 8

Approaching the summit

We're going to drop the code-sign for the little jumping man from now on. Look out for jumps just the same—there are plenty of thirds, fourths, fifths and even sixths about!

AAARGH!! IT'S MOVED!!

This is the feeling you sometimes gets when sight-reading. You're going along doing well—or so you think—and then one of the hands moves miles away and you panic —"Aaargh! Where am I now?" Then you must re-adjust your mind and carry on. Think how much **easier** it would be if you looked through the piece (especially if it's a short one) and **checked these things before you started!**

1

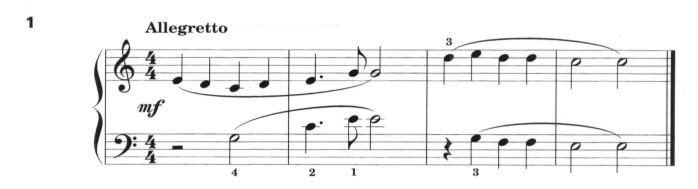

2

3

If you don't know the notes here, look at the previous bar and make an intelligent guess.

4

5

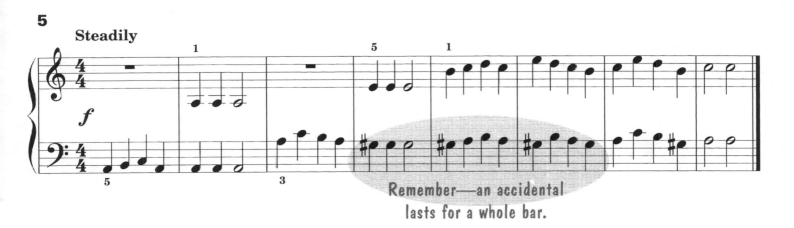

Remember—an accidental
lasts for a whole bar.

Keep going!

You're doing fine!

You might think that it's cheating to play a piece of
sight-reading more than once. But this isn't so, and you can still
go on improving your sight-reading even though you have played the
piece before. You will find that your sight-reading will improve steadily,
so do go back and play all the stages of this book over and over again!

B·E·A·T T·H·E G·R·E·M·L·I·N·S

Musical (or not so musical) gremlins have been at work on this page. They have moved and altered things, so that many of them are now wrong.

Can **you** put everything right?

Draw a ring round anything that is wrong and write the correction underneath.

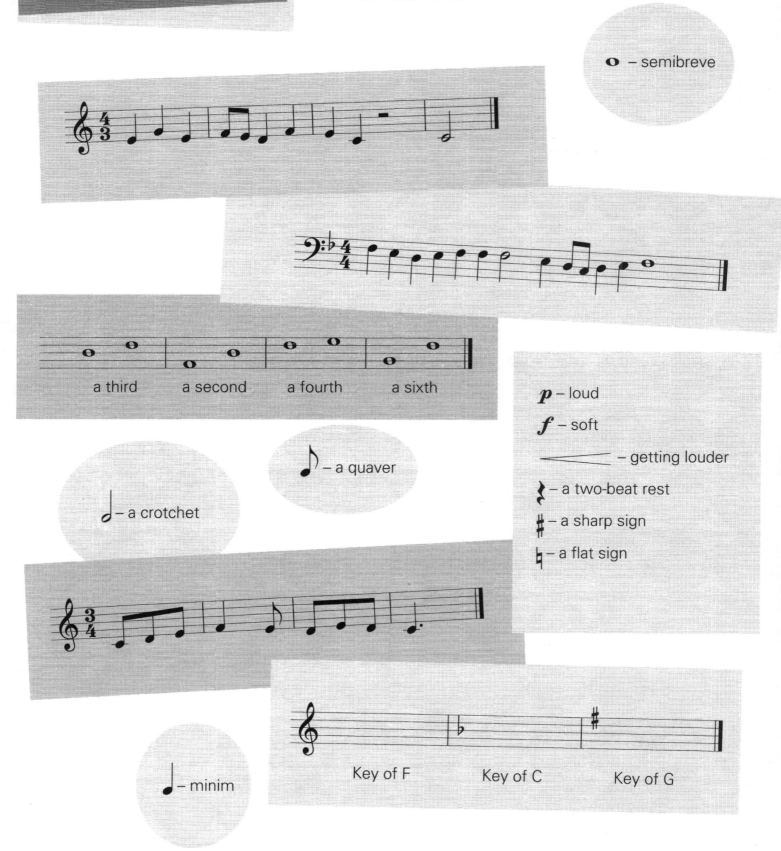

o – semibreve

a third   a second   a fourth   a sixth

p – loud

f – soft

— getting louder

— a two-beat rest

– a sharp sign

♮ – a flat sign

♩ – a quaver

♩ – a crotchet

♩ – minim

Key of F   Key of C   Key of G

On top of the world

Now we are going scale-wise.

Obviously, the first piece here has a scale of C, but what about the next piece? Are there any sharps or flats you might forget while trying to remember the fingering?

1

2

3 **Dolce**

4 **Allegretto**
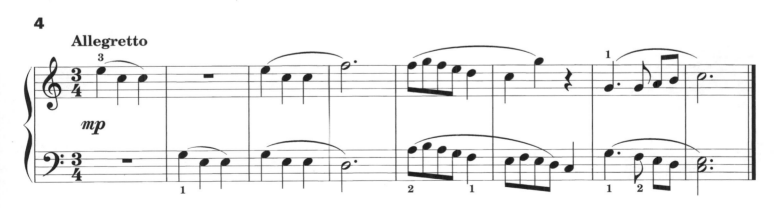

Printed by
Halstan & Co. Ltd., Amersham, Bucks., England

5

All the secret code-signs which you have collected on your journey have shown you how to spot and deal with the obstacles that are placed in your way when sight-reading. Don't forget the golden rule—COUNT! GO STEADILY! NEVER LOOK BACK!

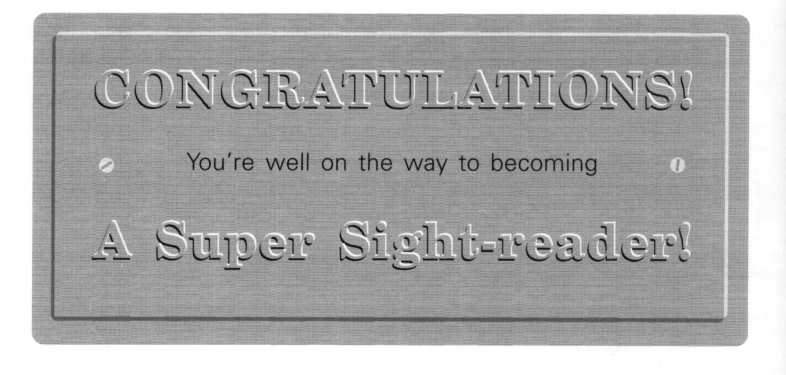

CONGRATULATIONS!

You're well on the way to becoming

A Super Sight-reader!

_____
NAME

_____   _____
TEACHER'S SIGNATURE   DATE